Purchase copies on the Web. www.amazon.com

Visit the Author at: **www.StephenPaulWest.com**

LIBRARY OF CONGRESS CATALOGING-IN-PUBLICATION DATA

West, Stephen Paul
Sexual Issues and Depression
Stephen Paul West
p. cm.

Summary: Depression show up in the heart and mind, and often disrupt our sexual behaviors. Here is a short work that explores the meaning of sexual issue during depression and how to find a cure.

Sex and Depression

Your Power to Cure Depression

Stephen Paul West

Hi. Welcome to my series of books analyzing all the symptoms of depression – and how those symptoms can be used to your advantage.

A madman ran me over and left me for dead on the side of the road. I had a long journey back from depression. Art was useful. Most of the artwork in these series is my original work.

I created the drawing above while recovering from injury. It is me being run-over as I walked my dog. The person drove down into the ditch, smashed his truck into my face, and fled the scene.

He left me for dead. He never hit his brakes. He remains unfound. My body – once strong – was broken. Sexual behavior spun out of control. I learned how to heal, and to develop a healthier sexual life than I had even before the depression. I can help you answer a lot of questions, and these answers are POWER to heal.

However, it wasn't just my body, but my mind was damaged as well: 40% head trauma and a damaged temporal lobe changed me sexually. A careless drunk sent me to the darkest depths of psychotic depression – but I crawled out of that pit. My experience is one of despair and of victory. It is one of brokenness and of healing. I know my works will help you.

"Sexual Issues and Depression" is a skill builder to carve out happiness again from the cliffs of despair. You will do this even while **boldly** facing the reality of injury, loss and confusion. Why is this possible – because you and I together are on a mission to find a solution. We are a good team.

The key to a healing path is found in understanding the symptoms of depression that you utilize when you are sad. This book teaches you how to understand your own depression symptoms and therefore find the path to healing **and even happiness**.

.•.

TABLE OF CONTENTS

Contact the author at:
stephen@stephenpaulwest.com

CHAPTER 1

Sexual Issues and Depression

*"Passionate acts - amorous words and touch-
which arise in the heat of the moment during sex
cannot be measured – and are as strange as
dreams" – Kama Sutra 100 A.D.*

"Sex is part of nature. I go along with nature." –
Marilyn Monroe

WHY IS MY SEX LIFE BROKEN?

Even without an injury or depression, sexual issues are amazingly common for people. Minor ailments such as low level diabetes, or slight blood pressure, cause sexual disruptions to millions of people daily. However, *Sexual Issues and Depression* looks at two enormous factors that cause sexual disruptions – a physical injury and depression.

It is unrealistic to expect wounded people to achieve a high <u>quantity</u> of sex. During an injury, you are busy healing, and may have little energy for romance. Instead of expecting frequent sex, I encourage you to seek a higher <u>quality</u> of sex. The age old debate of quality versus quantity is specifically germane to those suffering depression based sexual issues. More on this later.

"Why is my sex life broken?" should yield an obvious answer if you have been injured. The physical injury naturally leads to depression. Depression gets in your head. The principle organs for sex are not the ones below the waistline.

The principle organ for good sex is behind the skull – that is, your brain is the biggest erogenous zone. However, once the brain is hungry for sex, it still relies upon the body to be able to respond. When people are injured, feeling pain, and the brain is clouded with depression, there are often too many barriers to performance. This is why I promote a deliberate focus on quality of sex, and not a frequent number of times.

I will help you figure out the reason you have this symptom of depression. I help you formulate a healthy plan of action to restore this gift in your life.

•●•

Also, sex does not always become less during depression. Since my audience is injured victims, some head injuries create hyper-sexuality. Certainly, if your sex habits have increased to the point where they are destructive then go see a doctor. However, my focus is more on diminished sexuality as that is the more frequent result of depression and injury.

•●•

My information on sex is blunt, truthful, and realistic. I do not have any problem discussing porn, masturbation, medication and other little sexual secrets in the context of self-help. My goal in being direct is to be clearly informative but not to be ribald. Writing good self-help means not being squeamish about honest discussion of sex.

I want you to understand the symptom of sexual dysfunction during depression. *Sexual Issues and Depression* does not just count the number of symptoms and then conclude if you have depression or not; unlike all the other depression diagnostic tools. This book is far more useful to the reader.

I carefully analyze each particular symptom of

depression – all based on the Beck Depression Inventory and National Institute of Health guidelines. Once you understand particular symptoms then you can see a pattern of need in your life.

The symptoms are pointing the way to a healing. Not everybody cries. Not everybody has isolation. Not everybody has rage. Not everybody with depression has sexual disruptions.

What does your symptom of sexual issues communicate? How can you listen to sexual issues, and formulate a plan of healing? Why is sex troubling for you now?

I help you analyze all of the questions you have now on this symptom, and present a very useful conclusion to managing sexual issues by chapter's end.

DECODING THE SYMPTOM OF SEX ISSUES

Sex Issues represent a need to prioritize energy needs during recovery. During depression, the mind often consumes all available energy in problem solving and healing. This does not leave energy available to regulate hormones, blood flow, and arousal. For single people it is important to find the harmony with your mind – and be social but celibate. Couples need to plan for intimacy and have open dialogues as you recover.

My very first goal is to establish reasonable expectations. One of the big problems with depression is it paints everything black. Even if your sex life is actually good, depression is likely to make you critical of your behavior. Did you know that almost 56.9% of single men and 50.2% of females, age 18 to 24 did not even have sex last year? No? That is the data from the Kinsey Institute. (Oh, for those of you doing the math between males and females and notice the delta between guys and gals: nothing weird here. My guess is the 6.7% difference is because women in that age group are having sex with older men – that is why the percentages are not the same.) Still the average is 50+% of single people are celibate all year.

Well, it just goes to show that our expectations are often unrealistic. It might feel like everybody is having a sexual free-for-all, but the reality is that sex without love is not ideal – and finding love is difficult. So, single people are <u>not</u> having sex all willy-nilly.

Sexual Issues and Depression is very practical. My recommendation for single people recovering from an injury and depression is not to stress if you are celibate. You need your energy to heal from an accident and to cure the resultant depression. Most of the world is celibate anyway.

It is not fair to yourself or others to throw yourself into dating and sexual relationships when you are recovering from depression. Take a relationship sabbatical. Do not judge yourself. Enjoy being single. Masturbate to release sexual tension as it is a sure thing, no pressure, and healthy for endorphins and chemicals. Over 70% of males and 60% of women masturbate regularly from puberty until death. Even after 70+ years over 33% of women report solo masturbation. It is human, zero stress, and zero pressure. The most important step at this time is to recover from accident based depression – romance will find you on its own terms once you are ready.

•●•

However, partner relationships need to be able to survive your depression. Sex is an important mortar holding most relationships tightly together. *Sexual Issues and Depression* respects the importance of preserving your relationship during recovery from an accident. It is not fair to unilaterally deny your partner sexual satisfaction as you pick through your injury. I will speak more to partners, as a forced celibacy causes problems.

> "I divorced my husband because I was in a sexless marriage." Her eyes flashed with rage.

> "What does that even mean? Sexless? How is that possible." This blind date immediately jumped to some heavy discussion. Not your usual 'what do you do for a living' kind of a talk.

> "I will never be neglected like that again! Do you have a problem with that?" She challenged me with a flash on her cheek and a raised brow.

> "No problem. I still don't have any idea what you mean though. What is a sexless marriage anyway? Doesn't seem possible."

Turns out, I was clueless. Sexual depression makes for a dark and dangerous dating life.

The most important information I provide is truth that you can use. Depression negatively shades our reasonable expectations of life. People want a brass ring. Life just does not hand out brass rings, and it is easier to recover from depression with realistic goals.

I look at the physical, mental, and spiritual reasons for sexual issue caused by depression. You will understand your symptoms and be able to build healthy expectations for sex that includes your partner's well-being.

The Body and Sex Issues

Let me start by setting clear expectations. Just what is good sex anyway? What is '*normal*' and reasonable to expect relative to the rest of the world?

Breakdown by location ⇕	Country ⇕	Search Term = "SEX"	
	■ Poland	11.9% (3,614,105)	
	▦ United States	8.1% (2,470,958)	
30,400,000	▦ India	7.9% (2,407,623)	
Avg. monthly searches	▦ Turkey	6.9% (2,105,035)	
	▦ Vietnam	6.2% (1,896,823)	
	▦ Other countries	58.9% (17,905,456)	

Ad group ideas	Keyword ideas				⬕
Ad group (by relevance)	Keywords	Avg. monthly searches	Competition	Suggested bid	Ad impr.
Keywords like Se...	Sex	⮝ 30,400,000	Low	$0.26	

Explicit commentary lathers us in sticky fantasy until we are tainted from exposure. The graphic above shows we search 30 million times a month for the word 'sex'.

However, what is portrayed in media is not a reliable benchmark for sexual happiness. The media exposure to sex is waaaaAAAY beyond any normal human behavior. The media-bias results in exposure to sex about 4.4 times an <u>HOUR</u>!

It is unfortunate that people healing from injury, television viewing might be the only activity possible – and then you get sexually provoked beyond superhuman strength. This is truly unnatural and unhealthy and not even close to reality. The majorities of people are much more protective of their sexual health then is on display on television.

"Sexual content appears in 64% of all TV programs; those programs with sexual content average 4.4 scenes with sexually related material per hour. Talk about sex is found more frequently (61% of all programs) than overt portrayals of any sexual behavior (32% of programs). Approximately 1 of every 7 programs (14%) includes a portrayal of sexual intercourse, depicted or strongly implied."

-PEDIATRICS Vol. 114 No. 3 September 1, 2004

So, let me provide some hard research data on what is "*normal*" in sexual behavior.

Among couples in relationship the average number of times, various age groups have sex weekly*:

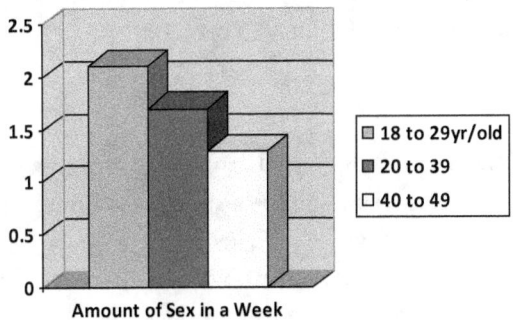

- 2.1 times a week for 18-29 year olds.

- 1.7 times a week for 30-39 year olds.

- 1.3 times a week for 40-49 year olds.

*based on Mosher, Chandra & Jones; *Advanced data from vital and health statistics*; no 362. Hyattsville,

MD: National Center for Health Statistics. 2005

You can see that the world is pretty tame. Do not get confused by the wild amount of sex portrayed in our media.

Some people might have sex daily. Some people might be celibate. Certainly, if you are injured, and depressed, gathering up enough energy for sex might be difficult. Here you can see that if you have sex once or twice a week or so, you are average for <u>HEALTHY</u> human sex frequency. Now, this data is based on people who have not been injured and do not have depression.

Obviously, if you have health issues then sex once or twice a week might be a stretch goal. Actually, I do not want you to make yourself do anything against your will. I just want you to have the information so you can decide when you are better. Avoid judging yourself too harshly compared to television and the media.

Did this help take some pressure off you? Do you think you can manage a great moment of sex about once or twice a week?

Do you think you can share this information with

your partner and see if that frequency is all right? Good sex once a week is sooOOO much better than a lot of crappy sex. Who cares what TV is depicting in the *'sex-sells'* commercialization of empty, meaningless and disease-risky behavior. I do not care. You do not care.

The data for once or twice a week is based on healthy, uninjured people. This information is not a law, but just a friendly guideline to help you on the road to recovery.

Good sex once or twice a week would make you about normal!

What is even better is that you and your partner get to decide what is good sex. For example, many couples like mutual masturbation. The naughtiness of the moment is enticing. This might be a great place to start if some injury has made other more robust sex out of the question during recovery. Other couples might have some other important imagery or play that is exciting. It is all up to you to define good sex!

●●●

Don't assume you and your partner both agree about your sex life during depression. You need to ask your partner if they are happy with the frequency and quality of the sex. You also need to ask them what might be a creative solution to closing the gap between desire and actuality. If your partner gets to help decide the issue, then they are more likely to stay happy (and therefore monogamous and supportive). If you take away partner's say in their own sexual expectations, you create additional stress and this negatively impacts your recovery.

While I am at it, let's talk about performance. I have established that having sex once or twice weekly as normal sex, but what IS normal performance during that moment.

How long do couples last during sex? What is normal for orgasms? What is normal sexual performance? There is so much pressure to be some kind of marathon runner of romance and often those incorrect assumptions create sexual frustration.

What is normal sexual performance for people?*

- Average vagina depth from opening to cervix is 2.46 inches and the average penis length is 5.8 inches. Naturally, some women and some men are on the far ends of average. But overall men have 2x more penis than vaginal depth.

- This means penis enlargement spam can be ignored; depressed males do not need to add an unhealthy body image. Nearly all men have enough penis already.

VAGINA DEPTH VS PENIS LENGTH

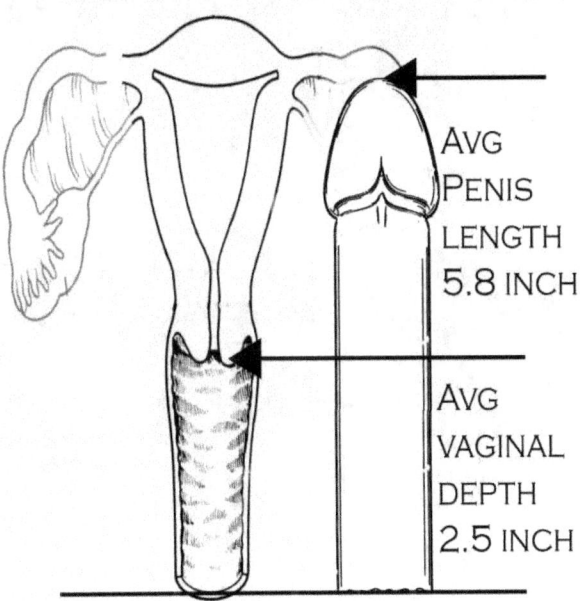

AVG PENIS LENGTH 5.8 INCH

AVG VAGINAL DEPTH 2.5 INCH

- However, to make a woman orgasm requires SIX different types of touch during sex for 80% of women to orgasm – caress the face... interlock the fingers. It is not the penis, so much as technique, that will satisfy most women. My advice here to men would be show love, be love, express love.

- 75% of men and 29% of women always have orgasms with their partner.

- 5.4 minutes is average time for men to ejaculate from moment of vaginal insertion. Anything under 2 minutes in duration is a common cutoff for premature ejaculation. This goes back to spending some time with touching technique on a woman. Learn how to touch, fondle, kiss and caress a woman in order to have high quality sex.

- Average sexual duration from fore-play to orgasm is twelve minutes.

- 13% of married couples reported having sex a few times per year, 45% reported a few times per month, 34% reported 2-3 times per week, 7% reported 4 or more times per week, and 1% report no sex for the last year.

*Most of this data is extracted from The Kinsey Institute of Health. See: kinseyinstitute.org

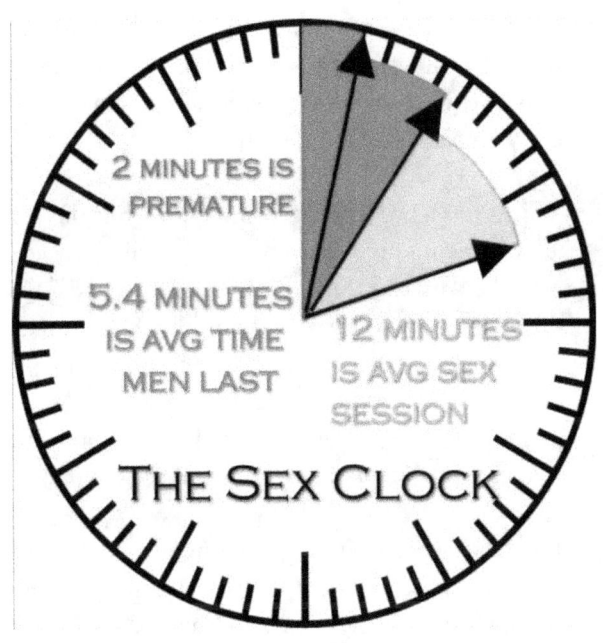

There is a universal need for people to feel normal – but it is our slight differences that make us exciting. The need for normalcy is even greater when we are depressed. However, my point in disclosing what is normal for sexual behavior is not to make you slavishly fixated on the numbers.

My point is for a depressed individual recovering from an injury to see that the actual benchmark for normal it is much lower than otherwise guessed. It is certainly much lower than what the media depicts in standard programming. So normal is about twice a week and 12 minutes a pop. No need to be depressed about not having crazy long sex every single day.

This is not a book on sex techniques – but there is a lot of technique to read between the lines. If you read the data you see about 25% of men and 71% of women have sex that does not lead to orgasm. It is normal to have sex for reasons other than a hurried sprint to the orgasm finish line. Many people enjoy sex just to be in the moment, celebrate life, unwind, and feel connected.

For example, even though the number of female orgasms were low at 29%, among women currently in a partnered relationship, 62% say they are very satisfied with the frequency and consistency of orgasm. The same data reported that women almost always orgasm during solo masturbation – so if you're female and can't come during masturbation there is definitely some kind of sexual barrier at this time.

A quick synopsis of the data indicates that normal

sexual behavior for partners is:

- Once or Twice a week for sex depending on age.

- Sex lasts about 12 minutes long.

- Guys average about 5.4 minutes before they come.

- Couples have orgasms 75% of the time for men and 29% for women.

- Adding mutual and solo masturbation to sex greatly improves orgasm rate.

- Most people are satisfied with their sex life at these normal levels.

Now that I have established some obtainable goals, I would like to move on to the barriers to sex during depression.

●●●

For the readers of *Sexual Issues and Depression* the physical barriers are very real, and I cover the most pressing (but medical doctors are good at helping in this area and I recommend a doctor's visit too!)

There is nothing earth shaking in the symptom of sexual issues during depression. The symptom of sexual issues is most likely teaching you:

- Anti-Depressants can totally switch off the body.

- Physically you cannot perform because of blood-flow and hormonal disruptions resulting from the injury.

- Your body is protecting every ounce of energy to aid recovery. Energy is redirected from sex into healing.

- Self-worth and sexuality are absolutely the same thing. Depression interferes with self-worth on a 24 and 7 basis and this impacts the body's ability to become aroused.

Most of these are physical issues and I address them in this section. Self-worth is a mental and spiritual matter that I discuss later in the appropriate sections.

First, anti-depressants can absolutely switch your body off sexually. Serotonin reuptake inhibitors (SSRI) such as Zoloft, Prozac, Paxil, Lexapro and many other SSRI meds are reported to suppress sex drive in up to 80% of questioned patients. There is a huge disconnect between "*the word on the street*" and clinical studies and FDA warnings about SSRI and sexual side-effects, as noted in one study:

> "The incidence of antidepressant-induced sexual dysfunction is difficult to estimate because of the potentially confounding effects of the illness itself, social and interpersonal co morbidities, medication effects, and design and assessment problems in most studies. Estimates of sexual dysfunction vary from a small percentage to more than 80%. This article reviews current evidence regarding sexual side effects of selective serotonin reuptake inhibitors (SSRIs). Among the sexual side effects, most commonly associated with SSRIs are delayed ejaculation and absent or delayed orgasm. Sexual desire (libido) and arousal difficulties are also frequently reported, although the specific association of these disorders to SSRI use has not been consistently shown."

- Effects of SSRIs on Sexual Function: A Critical

It was also dryly noted that since SSRI suppress male premature ejaculation that might be a good thing. Well, perhaps – but that's kind of being overly-positive don't you think?

It also seems that the sexual dysfunction from SSRI medications happens immediately, but it takes nearly two weeks before the medication helps with depression. This can be frustrating.

Still, going off SSRI meds is not a correct plan if you get the side-effect of sexually disinterested from these meds. The proper plan of action is to talk with your doctor about switching to another medication that might not have the libido impact.

Next, it is important to realize that the accident has most likely disrupted your chemistry. Erectile dysfunction is neither embarrassing nor uncommon. In fact, nearly one in three men report they lose their erections when putting on condoms.* Unlike depressed men, these are healthy males and not men who were smashed up in combat, auto accidents or other injuries:

- 28.1% of men reported that they had lost their erection while putting on a condom at least once during the last three times they used a condoms.

* The Kinsey Institute

Fortunately, for males there are several safe options such as Cialis, Viagra and Hormone patches that can correct blood pressure and hormonal disruptions. It is harder to '*see*' when a woman is having sexual problems because of the injury. However, women also have some options for low sex drive when hormonal deficiencies are found.

Let me be clear. Your brain is busy during depression. In trouble shooting mode it can '*forget*' to regulate testosterone and blood pressure. The hippocampus area is struggling during depression – and this is where biological regulation happens. It is highly valuable to you in a partnered relationship to talk to your doctor about medications that improve blood pressure and hormones. Wouldn't it be nice to fix the symptom of sexual dysfunction during depression without making your partner feel troubled? Sometimes, the solution is as easy as Cialis.

Get your motor running. Talk to your doctor.

I am not a doctor – but I am pretty sure you have one nearby. I know finding one that you are comfortable discussing depression and sexual issues might be tricky. Keep looking until you find the right doctor for you. Then **talk** to them about any sexual issues and **ask** them to help you improve your sex life. Quite often, the body corrects itself with just a short period on these medications.

•●•

Lastly, allow your body plenty of rest when recovering from an injury. I am not talking about just sleeping in one Saturday a month. You will need at least 8 months of deliberate, focused rest. Make yourself go to bed on time. Drop some of the crazy pressure in your life. Find a slower pace.

Finding a slower pace also includes NO sexual pressure. Right? I showed you that healthy people have sex between once and twice a week for about 12 minutes a session. Allow yourself a slower pace. Talk to your partner about how to make your sessions more exciting and fulfilling rather than shooting for meaningless high numbers.

I cannot say what is exciting to you and your partner. But some tricks I found include:

- Read something together and aloud that is exciting. A sex scene out of Harlequin romance novel? O, yeah!

- A surprising number of people like to watch their partner masturbate. In fact, for women it might be a great way for you to get in the mood for him, by taking some time alone an hour before you expect together time.

- Candles, flowers, a thoughtful note, a little gift and a warm shower are all just part of fore-play.

- Home baked goodies and a glass of wine add to a moment.

- Listen – really listen – to a couple of songs together. Talk about the lyrics.

- Give each other 10 minute shoulder and scalp and neck massage. Man, your neck is sore! So is your partner's. Take turns. 10 minutes each.

- Plan and budget some time. It's okay that sex isn't "spur of the moment and crazy passion." Really, it's okay to plan.

- Just add oral sex already. It's no biggie to surprise your partner with a few well-placed kisses – more if it's your thing.

- Lastly, say this aloud– "Every body type is a sexy body type."

So, decoding the symptoms of sexual issues has a

lot to do with energy and physical needs. If you are struggling with the symptom of sexual issues, there are solutions. The symptom is showing you that you need to take physical inventory and carefully manage the pressures in your life.

There is so much more to any symptom than just proof that you have depression! The symptoms are also telling you how to get better. No symptom is reflected in your body that does not actually demonstrate a path of healing. This includes sexual issues.

Once the physical requirements are met, you still need to consider the mental and spiritual aspects. However, I hope that by setting realistic expectations, and giving an honest view of normal sexual behavior, I help you on the path to healing.

The Mind and Sex Issues

I have no idea who first said, "*The brain is the most important erogenous zone*", but it's true. Sex starts in the mind. As a simple demonstration, I will return the fact that most people always orgasm when they masturbate. That act is about 10% manual stimulation and 90% mental erotica. You are, after all, having sex with yourself – so to speak. However, the reality is that you take your mind to whatever place you find exciting.

Since 94.3% of males and 84.6% of females age 25 to 29 report masturbating it's pretty safe to assume it's pleasurable. This also means many people are using their imagination a lot.

Sexual Issues and Depression has a great deal of information on how the mind enters into a problem solving mode during depression. This is a chemical and procedural change in the brain to induce logical solutions to the root cause of sadness.

> "Depression induces changes in body systems, producing effects that facilitate analytical rumination by reducing disruption. Specifically, depressed affect: (1) activates neurological mechanisms that promote attentional control, which gives problem-related information prioritized access to limited processing resources and makes depressive rumination intrusive, persistent, resistant to distraction, and difficult to suppress; (2) induces anhedonia, which reduces the desire to think about and engage in hedonic activities that could disrupt problem-related processing; and (3) promotes psychomotor changes that reduce exposure to stimuli that could disrupt processing (e.g., desire for social isolation, loss of appetite)."

> *- The bright side of being blue: Depression as an adaptation for analyzing complex problems -*

Andrews, P., et al; Virginia Institute for
Psychiatric and Behavioral Genetics

Please note that scientists know the brain changes
chemicals to suppress hedonistic pleasures. The
research states is thusly: *"Depression induces changes
in the body that…induces anhedonia, which reduces
the desire to think about and engage in hedonic
activity…"*

This is a fancy way of saying your brain changes
the chemicals so you do not spend time on fun,
when you should be problem solving. *"First, things
first,"* as my father used to say.

This chemical suppression of sex is one reason I
recommend single people actually embrace and
celebrate being single for a while. You can survive
a year without sex individually – especially if you
develop into a healthier and more confident
person during that year.

•••

However, a partnership may not be able to survive
a year of no sex. It is not possible for me to predict
if your relationship can withstand a sexual
sabbatical. However, if you do not even discuss

the issue with your partner's best-interests in mind, you violate the bond of trust that is necessary. Your partner very well might be struggling with your injury as well. Do not take away their free-will of self-expression by deciding they do not have ANY say in the matter. At least allow them to know you have a game plan for including their needs.

Again, your brain is deliberately suppressing the chemicals for fun and pleasure. This does not make you unloving or cold. Yes, you may not feel like having sex. But, your partner may not feel like being celibate. Since your mind is thinking in problem solving mode, you can put the logical thought in your head that your relationship must survive your depression. This is logical for self-preservation and you can accept this idea. If your brain is kind of blocking the idea of having fun, make it a logical decision instead. Simply veto your mind, and plan a nice time for sex. Your partner will feel better, and you will be surprised that you do as well.

The chemicals in your brain do not always know best during depression.

I feel like I need to re-iterate at this point that my book speaks to injured people. Obviously, if you are too hurt for the physical act of sex then that must be admitted and accepted. I hate positive thinking gurus who don't understand what it is to be injured. Four years after my hit and run, I developed a form of epilepsy. This affected my relationships. I understand you cannot just positively think away your injury.

So, I am encouraging couples to come to a workable plan to continue a reasonable sex life – but only to the extent that injuries allow. I am also encouraging celibacy for single people until they are healed enough for dating. It is possible that your symptom of sexual issues is letting you know that sex is no longer an option. In these cases, I strongly urge you to see a therapist who specializes in such debilitating injuries. There are 8 billion people in this world, so there are many ways to live a happy life – yours is but one.

The Spirit and Sex Issues

Sex is one of the strongest of biological forces. Its earthy power upon humanity falls in order just after air, food and water. However, we are much more than just the crude material of human needs. There is a divine spark within all of us. Each one of these earthy needs has a great deal of spiritual symbolism attached as well.

Air, for example, is a perfect symbol of the spiritual realm. Michael Angelo's *Sistine Chapel* depicts the common heavenly thread of air. God hovers in the sky so near to Adam that the two may touch if they both just stretch out their hands. It is easy to find spiritual stories in all religions about air, food, and water. Those forces are magical, mythical, and very divinely inspiring.

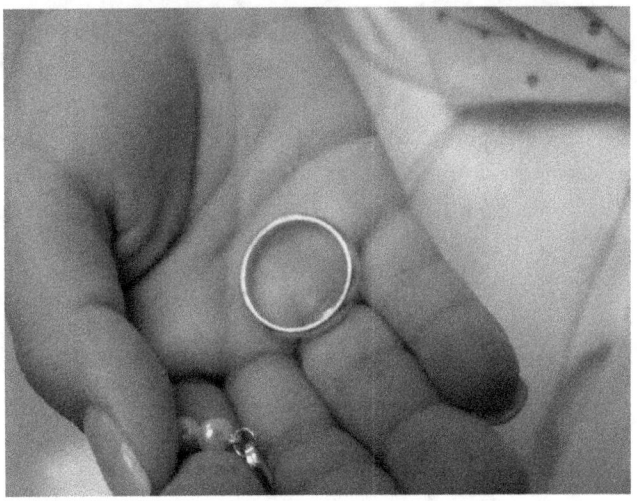

Sex is no different from air, food, and water. It also has a spiritual content that cannot be ignored. Sex and love are so tangled up in our psyche that the two words are substituted in conversations around the world; i.e. "*Love making*", "*Let's make*

love", etcetera.

But Love is spiritual. God is Love. So there is a God factor to be found in sex. Sex and Love are spiritual; just like Air and Heaven, or Water and Baptism, or Food and Communion.

Just we modern mortals get squeamish when we talk about God in our sex lives. Our ancestors had no such puritanical compunctions. Sex and God were historically woven into the same tapestry. "*Marriage is great, especially in bed!*" Hebrews 13:4

For a person decoding the symptoms of depression there is nothing more important than finding a place of love, healing, and understanding – this includes your sex life.

Consider for a moment that there is junk food and good food. There is also junk sex and good sex. There is love and then there is sex. Sex without love is a counterfeit of all the true potential of moment. Certainly, it might satisfy an ache of biological need – just as a gas-station burrito might fill a gut. But loveless sex cannot fill a person like a great Thanksgiving dinner can fill hunger.

Ignoring the loving component of sex is a denial

34

of a spiritual component of yourself; and therefore sex is more rewarding in a loving environment. There is an entire book of the Bible devoted to passionate love making – and Semitic scholars teach this book is symbolic of God and humankind. But here is a sampling of what kind of wonderful sex is available!

The Song of Songs, which is Solomon's

Kiss me with kisses: for love is better than wine.

My husband told me, "Look! You are beautiful, my love; you are beautiful; eyes like doves."

He slipped his left hand is under my head, and embraced his right hand beneath my waist. He pulled me into him.

He said, "Rise up, my love, my fair one, and run away with me. Winter is done. The rain is over and gone. Flowers grow upon the earth when I'm with you. The birds are singing and the dove's coo when I have you in my bed. You are my springtime! You are so pretty, my love; there is no spot on you! You ravish my

35

heart with one of your eyes. A single jewel on your neck makes my heart beat fast!

"Our love is better than wine and your lips," he moaned my name, "Your lips are as sweet as honey. Honey and wine are under your tongue when we kiss; and you, woman - my pretty wife - are like a spring shut up, a fountain sealed."

My husband poured some wine in my navel, and sipped it like I was a living goblet. He kissed beneath my goblet and whispered, "Your thighs are fine! The best jeweler made your hips out of pure gold. Your body is my favorite tree. I want to climb your branches and shake you. Your breasts are like fruit, and I'll nibble at them."

I whispered into my husband's ear; "Yeah, my love. Go up into this tree. Shake my branches until my fountains flows. My kisses are so intoxicating you will sleep like a babe when I'm done with you."

I am my beloved's, and his desire is toward me.

I am not a Bible scholar, but I recognize steamy love making when I read it! Anyway, this is the banquet of life.

●●●

Notice earlier that I talked about QUALITY of sex

life versus quantity. I truly hope you can recover from your injury quickly so that you can have a rewarding relationship; rich and haunting and passionate.

I realize that a broken body might hurt too much for vigorous sex. It is still important to restore a rewarding sex life at some level. Understand that a starving person needs calories; and even a little food is better than starvation. In a similar manner, you might be very limited in your romance, but still give time to your partner. Sex is not life or death like food and water. We can learn to adapt to its absence, and might need to do so for a while. What is very important is that your partner feels valued as you work your way through the injury.

Your injury cannot be all about yourself. Ironically, researchers discovered people recovered from depression faster when they do something kind and altruistic.

> "In the same year, Schwartz et al. focused on a sample of 2,016 members throughout the U.S. The study investigated whether altruistic social behaviors such as helping others were associated with better mental health. Questionnaires revealed that after adjusting

for variables, both helping others and receiving help were associated with positive mental health.

In fact, giving help was more significantly associated with better mental health than was receiving help. This study also emphasized that altruism must be reasonable for the giver in order to bring benefits. The authors found that "feeling overwhelmed by others' demands had a stronger negative relationship with mental health than helping others had a positive one"

- Schwartz, et al; Psychosomatic Medicine 65, 778-785 (2003) (heavy edits mine).

By including your partner, you make your recovery better – especially if you know your sex life will change dramatically. The studies all prove that giving help – as long as you do not feel taken advantage of, nor overwhelmed – significantly increase your health up to *"33 percent reduction rate in mortality for volunteers compared to nonvolunteers."*

•●•

I personally did not stop dating during my recovery period. It took me about 4 years (and counting) to manage my Traumatic Brain Injury (TBI). I dated up to three women a week while recovering from injury. Anybody in the romance game knows this is a lot of dating. In retrospect, this was foolish of me when I was struggling with TBI.

In that time, I gained – and lost – a fiancée. This was painful for me. Furthermore, it was certainly not her fault. My behaviors were erratic – and often irrational – as to make untenable a long term relationship. My place of depression was amazingly deep and tragic. I did not ask to be run over by a truck; but I had to live with the fallout of the injury entirely by myself.

So dating was something I figured out quickly because I was so lonely and depressed.

I figured out that adding sex to a casual dating relationship was unhealthy, unrewarding and – ironically – even a little more depressing. Yes, it sucks to be alone. Mindless sex will not help. Mindless sex is what masturbation is all about. That is safe, non-judgmental, disease free and a lot less complex than relationship based sex.

Despite what some controlling people might claim, there is no religious restriction in the Christian Bible against masturbation. (In fact, the word is not even in the Bible at all). Furthermore, the New Testament reports, *"Do you have faith? Great! Keep it to yourself before God. Happy is a person that doesn't condemn himself in the things which he does."* Romans 14:22. This message, of course, is to not judge yourself, or others, for being human. It could easily be applied to eating, drinking – and yes – even to masturbation.

I figured out that casual sex with mere strangers was unrewarding because the Spiritual aspect of Love was completely missing. I understand that a body will have cravings if you are single. In my opinion, those cravings for single people are best met with masturbation. This is especially good advice if you are a single person who is *Sexual Issues and Depression* . Since about 90% of all people admit to masturbating sometimes in their life, I am just saying aloud what people are doing behind closed doors anyway.

A soul can mess up a marriage when depressed.

The spiritual aspect of sex is why I advise single people to embrace celibacy during recovery from depression. There is no reason to add additional levels of complexity to your life. Your one and only job at this time is to recover successfully from an injury. Date if you choose – but be cautious about throwing yourself around in casual sex. Without Love you will find empty sex just makes your depression more profound.

Sex for couples must be discussed during recovery of an injury. I set real-world expectations earlier that prove most <u>healthy</u> people have sex slightly more than once a week. The quality of good and loving sex will meet a spiritual need. However, until the body is properly mended even this might be difficult. You cannot just deny your partner during this recovery period, though. Allow your partner – that other half of your spiritual journey – the right to participate in your pain and ultimate victory over your injury.

> *Sex Issues represent a need to prioritize energy needs during recovery. During depression, the mind often consumes all available energy in problem solving and healing. This does not leave energy available to regulate hormones, blood*

flow, and arousal. For single people it is important to find the harmony with your mind – and be social but celibate. Couples need to plan for intimacy and have open dialogues during recovery.

THE PITFALLS OF SEX ISSUES

Sexual disorders can be very frustrating. Certainly, sexual issues can greatly harm self-esteem. It is difficult to recover from depression if you have an issue that is harming your self-esteem.

There is a possible risk in a partnered relationship that the other member might resent lack of sexual attention. A worst case scenario of this neglect will result in infidelity. It is also possible you will be left alone.

You can see that the dangers of sexual issues may create an additional burden of heart-break during your recovery. The erosion of any relationship – as I experienced with a fiancée – has long reaching repercussion to your depression. I was able to regroup after my heart-break and take inventory. From my pain, I was able to write a creative analysis of Sexual Issues and Depression.

I sincerely want you to overcome any sexual issues. I strongly urge you to see your doctor for physical problems. Get any treatment necessary. Make certain you talk with your partner about your plans for restoring a rich and rewarding sexual life. Even it if takes a few years, a good partner is understanding and supportive.

THE STRENGTH OF SEX ISSUES

This book teaches you that each individual symptom of depression is teaching you a path of healing. I hope that by this far into the book you agree with this idea. Your symptoms are not just making you *'sad'*. Your symptoms are demonstrating an emotional, physical, and physiological need. Your symptoms are trying to process the pain to make you happy again.

So, sexual issues are teaching you that your energy is out of balance.

You do not have enough energy to have intimacy with another person. Since partnered sex is a give and take environment, sexual issues show that your body and mind are not ready for give and take.

Fortunately, lack of sex will not kill you. This is why a single person should embrace celibacy during the healing from injury. Do not stress about Hollywood's uncouth message about *"getting laid."* Hedonism is a pathetic example of sex.

Partnered relationships are healthier for people. It is important that you preserve your relationship even during depression. You cannot make the injury entirely about yourself if you have somebody else in your life. Your partner needs to have their voice heard in finding a solution to intimacy issues.

There are medical conditions that can interfere with sex. These are the easiest things to conquer as all you need to do is TALK with your doctor. Cialis and Viagra, for example, are drugs that jump start a male libido, and after a while are often not needed at all. Hormonal imbalances for women can be treated medically as well. Blood pressure issue also can disrupt the arousal reflex.

•••

Positive plan with the symptom of sexual issues:

1. Doctor's appointment specifically about sexual issues if it's that noticeable.

2. Set a realistic goal for intimacy – typically once or twice a week is normal.

3. If you are single, celibacy is a great plan during recovery from depression. Date if you wish, but only enter into a sexual relationship when you are healthy and feel capable of giving and receiving love.

4. Couples need to talk together and develop a workable solution to intimacy.

5. Mutual masturbation is a common

technique to make intimacy rewarding.

6. Include time for romance and plan to have the energy.

7. Cialis or Viagra for men. Hormonal treatments for women often help.

8. Do not just retreat into silence as that is not healthy.

9. Sexual quality is SO much better than worrying about how often you have sex a week. Focus on making your intimacy as high quality as possible.

Sex Issues represent a need to prioritize energy needs during recovery. During depression, the mind often consumes all available energy in problem solving and healing. This does not leave energy available to regulate hormones, blood flow, and arousal. For single people it is important to find the harmony with your mind – and be social but celibate. Couples will need to plan for intimacy and have open dialogues during recovery.

CHAPTER 2

Unraveling the Mystery of Depression

"I am now the most miserable man living. Whether I shall ever be better I cannot tell; I awfully forebode I shall not; To remain as I am is impossible; I must die or be better." - Abraham Lincoln January 23, 1841

DEPRESSION (1): a state of feeling sad: dejection (2): a psychoneurotic or psychotic disorder marked especially by sadness. -Noah Webster's Dictionary 2011

•••

THE EBB OF HUMAN DEPRESSION

Depression pours from human eyes. It just will not leave. You fight and fight, and it just digs in deeper and deeper.

Well, this book explains to you the importance of

tears during depression. Healing comes from understanding.

●●●

I remember putting up my hand as the shadow closed in on me. After that — I was never the same again.

The 2 ton black shadow devoured me, striking me fully in the right side of my body – and crushing my skull into my brain. The force tore my brain stem at the base of my left temporal lobe. The driver left me for dead. He remains unfound to this very day.

My personal struggle with depression has roots in a physical injury. Depression did not just sneak into my life. It kicked the teeth from my head and setup a shop of torment as weird and wicked as the wicked brain injury inside my skull.

Depression savaged my mind, tormented my soul and did not care a bit about my pain. My sorrow. My confusion.

I crawled out from under that crushing weight. I fought back. I learned...I learned the very weakness of depression. I found that the very trick to slaying depression was using its own symptoms against it.

And so will you.

•●•

This short book is a part of a series of short works that look at all the symptoms of depression.

Sexual Issues are universal when people feel sorrow... but we also cry when happy, or even cutting onions.

Sexual Issues are easily recognize, but it also is confusing for the deeply depressed. When we need the most comfort in our life we mess up our sexual life – sometimes drive people away. Often we make horrible choices to try and make up for missed opportunity. People see too deep and know too much; but don't know what to do.

My works focus on assisting people cure depression that may, or may not, be based on a physical injury. I am not a medical doctor and need to remind you to seek a doctor's help in your fight to overcome sorrow. My goal is to help you, and not push away any healthy solution – even regular ol' medical ones.

51

The surprising answer to banishing depression is found in the very symptoms you display. Symptoms of depression are not just gigantic pains in the heart. These symptoms are also the cure – but only if you learn what they mean.

I identify the symptoms and analyze them in great detail.

If you want to cure your depression, you must first understand your symptoms. Certainly, many medications can keep you from showing signs of depression, but that does not mean your body has processed the pain.

I found that we are often merely treating the symptoms and not finding a cure. In fact, masking the symptoms often makes the depression GROW.

- The cure was what I needed.
- The cure is what I found.
- The cure is in these pages.

I look carefully into the reasons for tears, eating disorders, dreams, rage, isolation, fatigue, confusion, addiction, sex issues, and dark thoughts. These are the core symptoms of depression. I look carefully at all these symptoms and find the whispering need within the human soul. Tears? Yes…they are speaking to us. Anger? Even that raging lion is still whispering a need – perchance a cure for those who listen closely.

Well, listen I did, and what did I find?

I found that all the symptoms of depression tell me the cure to a need! **Tears whisper what the body wants.** Rage shouts what the soul needs! Isolation screams a silent chant of information.

But all the time we are taught to ignore all that information. Fight the tears; hold back the rage; run from the isolation. We deliberately sedate the great doctor within and mask all the symptoms. This only makes depression darker, less enlightened, and more feared.

Am I not telling the truth?

What does your own heart say right now?

Are your sexual issues your enemy?

Or, is your body trying to tell you something?

Answer that riddle and you find the power in my

book.

I taught myself to respect the symptoms as beneficial and informative. Some guy crushed me with a car – and took away my happiness; but I overcame horrible, injury based depression.

~Your tears and fatigue.
~Your isolation and rage.
~Your appetite change and dreams
~Your confusion and addictions
~Your sex issues and dark thoughts.

~All Symptoms.
~All Solutions.

Your physical symptoms of depression are not the cause <u>of depression</u>, but rather a biological manifestation showing you a way of healing from depression.

Instead of making war on the symptoms, this pioneering book teaches you to make those symptoms valuable allies; and in so doing you vanquish the tyrant of depression by assimilating it into your essence.

Depression will not rule you. You will rule depression.

•●•

The reality is that the crying is a normal symptom of depression. And symptoms of depression are a normal and NECESSARY part of human behavior. We all need to weep, we all need to be isolated from time to time, we all need rage, and we all – every one of us – have dark thoughts on a regular basis.

Many books use defeatist attitudes such as "dealing with depression", "living with depression", or "coping with depression". This is not a healthy mindset as it puts the emotion of depression <u>over</u> the identity of the person. I say no! I am not a slave to depression! Instead, I teach a healthy approach is to be in <u>harmony</u> with your depression.

Making war with depression symptoms is a losing proposition.

However, I truly believe you can and WILL have a vibrant recovery. This is my absolute goal in writing this self-help book.

<u>Sexual Issues and Depression </u>teaches you the benefits of the symptoms of depression. It teaches

55

you the importance of a particular symptom as being a path of healing. It is normal and even healthy to have symptoms of depression – especially when something horrible happens in your life. The symptoms only become unhealthy when they dominate your identity. You will always have symptoms of depression as you NEED to both express and heal from hurt. However, you cannot become a slave to the whims of sadness. Your symptoms, when properly understood, become valuable tools in making you whole. You are not 'coping', 'dealing with', or 'living with' depression; rather you are expressing, processing, and healing yourself from sorrow.

Your body requires the symptoms of depression in order to recover from the hard blows of life. It is only when the symptoms rule us, or we fear to process the symptoms correctly, that we become pathologically depressed.

This book empowers you to master your symptoms in a positive manner. You will be stronger, I promise.

●●●

The prop blast of the helicopter blades shook me to life. The pressure of the wind snapped me out of my unconsciousness. The turbulence attacked me on all sides.

"Buddy. Buddy!" A pilot in full-helmet and goggles leaned over the top of my face. The roar of the blades pushed tears from my eyes. "Buddy, what happened?"

"Are we at war?" I asked without any idea of my name, where I was – or any answer to 'what happened' in my mind.

I then heard the sickening crunch of the truck smashing into my body — a full half-hour after I was run down in cold blood. Some kind of twisted auditory trick my brain played as it tried to put itself back in order. I felt the inky black swallow me up again like a hot and angry predator.

I was out cold.

•●•

Many books and medical treatments of depression imply that sorrow is a faceless, unconquerable ambiguity that is unknowable, and therefore, an incurable illness. My book changes all this. Read on to discover your path of healing! Read on to conquer your depression!

Not much has changed in popular definition of depression as a medical condition of sadness in the last two hundred years. It has a bit more medical jargon attached to it, and it has moved up a bit in Mr. Webster's dictionary, but we are just as far from finding a "cure" as our ancestors.

Perhaps we are even farther from healing depression than our ancestors. Our modern interactions are too friable and too callously brief. Information flows as a crushing tumult with ceaseless and suffocating pressure. The simple harmonies of nature are far removed by the clattering cacophony of our technology. In the end, we drift far from the shores of happiness. Modern life is a rip-tide of denial pushing us ever away from the healing shores of empathy and healing.

Our ancestors seemed to have more patience with each other in this matter of profound sadness. They seemed more willing to listen, help, and comfort. The Internet might be great for information, but it is a heartless beast for compassion.

Take, for example, that Abraham Lincoln suffered his entire life with crushing depression and yet was elected President (and it was widely known he was melancholy and he still won election).

In fact, Lincoln was often so despairing that friends would remove all guns and knives from him during his dark periods for fear he might harm himself. "Hypo" or "Melancholy", he called it. His gift for words painted a sad canvas that we easily relate to, as I quoted in the opening header:

> "I am now the most miserable man living. Whether I shall ever be better I cannot tell; I awfully forebode I shall not; To remain as I am is impossible; I must die or be better."
>
> -January 23, 1841, Lincoln; Letter to John T. Stuart,

Abraham Lincoln was not alone in depression.

You are not alone in depression.

- Royalty like King Solomon and Princess Diana;
- Movie Stars like Marilyn Monroe and Harrison Ford;
- Musicians like Beethoven and Eminem;
- Painters like Jackson Pollock and Degas;

- Politicians like Winston Churchill and our Mr. Lincoln;
- Authors like Hemmingway and J.K. Rowlings;
- Specialists in comedy like Chris Farley and Robin Williams – are afflicted!
- And so is every person on the face of the earth.
- Rich and poor.
- Healthy and sick.

All will face, the faceless creature called depression.

And yet depression remains an uncured mystery? Why?

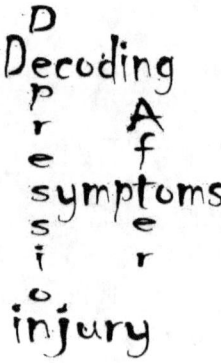

It is cruel irony that something ubiquitous to every human being is foreign to each of us. It would seem that great thinkers would have long ago solved depression. Yet, it remains perhaps the greatest challenge of our modern era.

Not only does depression tenaciously reside, but also it still perplexes the medical community. Why does depression affect some people much more intensely than others? How can a person find happiness again?

.•.

Nobody asks more questions than the depressed.

"Why am I crying? Why am I so angry all the time? Why am I fatigued? Why, why, why?"

The purpose of this book is to help the heartbroken – the melancholy as Lincoln wrote – to decipher the cryptic symptoms of depression. The knowledge of your symptoms unlocks the hidden path to restoration of health!

Consider for a moment these two depressed individuals. I will return to them in a bit, but for now, I just want you to think about them:

<u>Person A Exhibits Symptoms of:</u>
Tears
Recurrent Dreams
Fatigue

~versus~

<u>Person B Exhibits Symptoms of:</u>
Rage
Isolation
Addiction

Are these people the same?

Are they even close to having the same needs?

Most definitely not. The two individuals above have a markedly different set of symptoms; a different set of "Why do I…?" However, medically they are lumped together under a broad diagnosis of "Depression".

However, the different set of Why's reveal a different set of needs, and subsequently a different <u>path</u> for healing from depression. Most importantly, both of these individuals can become happy again, if they learn to meet the demands of their unique symptoms of depression.

The symptoms are telling these two individuals how to heal from the blow of depression. The symptoms are the "clotting, scabbing and scarring" of the invisible wound of depression. Depression symptoms are unique to each person because our individual needs are unique. Diagnosing every symptom under one umbrella of "depression" is exactly like diagnosing every bodily injury as "physically hurt". Cuts are different from bruises, which are different from broken bones. Each specific injury has its own physical symptom that demonstrates the body's way of healing physical injury.

Simply put, the solution to healing your depression is decoding your symptoms. Solving the puzzle of the "WHY" of your behavior of depression gives you powerful insight into dispersing the sorrow you feel.

Why does one person cry? Why does one person withdraw? Why does another person have fatigue? Yet another has rage? Maybe one poor soul has all these symptom and still functions. Still another individual resorts to suicide without any outward demonstration of symptoms. Yet all these people are lumped under a generic description of "depression".

Unfortunately, it is this vague grouping of every symptom into an unrecognizable mess that prevents solving depression. By neglecting the various symptoms of depression, the medical community inhibits a healthy convalescence of depression.

However, I have found the key to deciphering the mystery of depression! I have unlocked the meaning of each symptom of depression and shine a light on a healing path!

This knowledge helped me greatly, and I am most happy to share my discovery. But first let me describe my experience.

This book is one in a series that explains the deep reason for each and every symptom of depression. This is not just a 'so what' moment. This is not just mere information – it is the power to transform. I hope this little book helps you find the power to be happy.

A Singular Incident Of Sorrow

I saw the black pickup round the curve in the distance. Its tires did not squeal. The vehicle was traveling normally between the lines. It looked… well… it looked safe.

My old dog, Bandit, walked over, sat in the ditch, and waited for the truck to pass us.

I got Bandit from the pound as a puppy and now he was ancient; a collie mix of some sort. He loved to walk with me. So it was just an old dog and me alone in the middle of nowhere Texas. There was never much traffic way out here anyway, so it wasn't a big deal. In fact, the black pickup was the first vehicle I've seen this morning.

I smiled at my clever old dog because he was wise enough to sit and wait for vehicles to pass safely. I bent over to pat head.

A shadow closed in on me.

This vehicle was no longer on the road. It was down in ditch with my dog and me. I reflexively put up a hand.

Too late.

The black shadow devoured me, striking me fully in the right side of my face.

On a breezy, clear Saturday morning on the back roads of Bastrop, Texas, the truck left the road.

The driver never hit the brakes. He never stopped even after he ran me over. He plowed the front of his late model, black Chevy truck into another human being. My blood splashed on the bridge sign twenty feet from where he hit me. My body was found in the middle of the road.

The driver left me for dead. He remains unfound to this very day. So, I drew the little tattoo below. It used to have little teeth flying out of my flattened skull – but that seem a bit redundant to me in art; even though it was a sad reality in the street.

Never hit his brakes? Why? I still wonder if it was not just a thrill hit for some sociopath. Tire paths in the grass lead right to me petting my dog in the ditch; but not a single brake mark to remind me that people might be basically good and just make mistakes.

The police actually spray painted around my body once they found me. I suppose they needed it for their investigation. In the future, that spray paint would remind me of exactly what happened that day.

But now they painted around my body, I was not really there though. I was busy in the silky-darkness picking up a monster called TBI – Traumatic Brain Injury – from a place where nightmares are made real.

TBI is this monster devouring one of us every 21 seconds.

It came to gobble me up one day.

Maybe now it comes for you.

If it comes, it brings crushing depression; that much I can testify.

My personal struggle with depression has roots in a physical injury. This work, "**Sexual Issues and**

Depression" is specifically focused on those who can identify a root cause of depression; that is, those who've had a physical injury.

Since my depression was so crushing and cruel, I am certain my work will also help people with general depression that just "happened" (such as teen depression, for example). My work is based on my injury and what I learned (and am still daily learning) from that accident – but in reality pain is the root of depression. I learned a lot about pain. And I learned to beat depression. So can you.

The fact of the matter is that injured people <u>cannot CHANGE</u> the situation. If a person loses an arm to an accident, wishing it did not happen does nothing to change the reality. The arm is always gone. A woman cut-to-shred in an auto accident has those scars as a daily reminder.

I have learned that the brain is greatly savaged in an accident. Perhaps the head injury will give you a form of epilepsy as it has done to me. I am uncertain if those mental injuries can ever fully dissipate.

People stop bleeding eventually, but something lingers of that wound always and forever in the person.

So, injured people are stuck with the situation that causes the depression. They cannot change the moment in time, which precipitated the loss. Instead, they must change their approach if they want to defeat depression. That is what my work teaches. It will teach you to analyze your symptoms and formulate a successful plan of recovery. The application of my approach requires the individual reader to explore and identify their symptoms. It requires you to heal yourself.

Instead of just lumping symptoms all together into depression, I found that each symptom has MEANING! There is a mystery to solve about how you process your depression.

●●●

If you solve the meaning of the symptom, you also uncover the path to healing! Not just living with depression, but also actually living <u>above</u> depression!

And one of the important points I noticed in favor of the depressed is we are VERY analytical. I am writing to a highly intelligent, highly motivated audience. Are you depressed? You bet! Are you reading everything you can in order to find an answer? You bet!

Depression is a horrible feeling, but I also know from experience that much benefit, power, and accomplishment can come from such a low place in our lives.

I help you to succeed because you are clever, you are searching, and you are reading this material closely. I feel very confident in my program; I was taught keenly of its value by life grinding me up. Moreover, I also have the utmost faith in my readers because depressed people are strong seekers of solutions.

I believe in you and I know that Sexual Issues and Depression will help you find happiness again.

IT WILL ALL BE OKAY – NOT REALLY!

Soldiers blasted to pieces in combat. Children crushed in bicycle accidents. People taking bone shattering falls. Victims mugged and shot. Diabetes taking a limb. Lupus taking everything.

None of these things will ever "be okay". They won't just "work themselves out." And the injured are not just magically, "gonna be all right." In fact, this kind of trite advice in the face of horrific loss is without any honesty. By minimizing the reality of the situation, it discounts the path of healing after suffering a horrific loss. To add insult to the injury, the wounded person is supposed to reply, "thanks, that really helps."

Naturally, it does not help even in the slightest.

Perhaps more honest advice is, "you shall overcome", "time heals all wounds", and "this too shall pass". At least these statements demonstrate that injury is major, and it takes energy and time to find equilibrium again.

I personally think the best advice is: "I'm sorry. What can I do to help?"

Work is much better than words!

However, when I was run over the common advice was, "just shake it off man!"

Let see, I had 40% head trauma from the right frontal lobe (coup injury) back around to my occipital lobe (countercoup). Shaking it off? Really? Shaking of ANY kind was most definitely not what I needed!

However, I do not want to make this a work on my particular injury of Traumatic Brain Injury (TBI). This work is about depression for any type of accident victim.

I should note that the brain injury left me vulnerable to depression in dimensions waaaAAAY beyond anything I'd experienced previously. I am now an expert in the extremes of depression symptoms because I experienced them from the agony of a dysfunctional mind – intense, without warning and often darkly despairing. Compounding matters, I come from a family of great people – but great people with tempers. My ancestors were soldiers in EVERY war they could entangle with life and limb. Obviously, my Irish, Norman, Polish and Ukraine temperament was a bit assertive – but I was dangerously aggressive (so much so that each time I was pulled over I ended up on the ground with an officer's gun pointed at my head).

From this phoenix of ruin, I harmonized with depression.

I know my experience with depression will greatly help you!

My symptoms of depression would strike me

without any warning and plunge me into really, really, dark places.

Suicidal thoughts?

You bet – and of the most violent kind. My shattered mind had little or no coping skills. Pithy advice like, "shake it off" refused to acknowledge my genuine and legitimate need for help.

I learned just to fake my health to avoid judgment from those around me. I even learned to lie to doctors because I could tell they did not care. I was also worried they might commit me to a State Hospital, and that would not have been helpful.

Fortunately, I eventually found two great doctors who laid the ground-work for recovery. These physicians rebuilt my shattered faith in the medical community. Together with my drive to figure out my behavior, I uncovered the mystery to mastering depression. However, it took me several years before I even found these great doctors that I could trust.

I was a ship without help during the darkest hours of my life.

I do not want you to be a little lost ship. May Sexual Issues and Depression be a lighthouse to your wandering soul.

• ● •

My life experience with injury based depression taught me two important things:

First, the depressed people feel emotions at a much higher degree than normal. I felt everything maybe 10X stronger than ever before in my life. I once told a doctor, "I have less emotional control then I did as a child." Even as I write, I am a man much more subject to pathos than before, but I am perhaps even a better man than I was before I got hurt. My injury has developed me, pounded me into a more empathetic person, and forged me in a furnace against depression.

Secondly, physical injury requires a person to find happiness despite the actual reality of the injury. Pithy statements are not enough magically to empower the injured. They need genuine <u>skills</u> to manage the reality of the loss.

Sexual Issues and Depression is a skill builder to find happiness again even while **boldly** facing the reality of your depression. Do not fear! You are smart enough to know yourself. This book gives you wonderful insight into getting yourself back on track to being positive, and even happy.

THE MYSTERY OF DEPRESSION DECODED

People demonstrate their deeply repressed personal needs in their individualized symptoms of depression. Yet, society (including doctors) carelessly lump every symptom of depression beneath the same dark umbrella. This careless treatment of the symptoms of depression makes a generic blob of the sorrow; and it is this featureless ambiguity that makes it an unknowable, and therefore, incurable illness.

This is not so. Depression is a knowable, and even a useful, human process. It not an inky blob but it has features – think of the features as "handles" that you can use.

See? The expression – "I can't get a <u>handle</u> on my depression" – drops away if you understand your symptoms. By analyzing how you personally process your pain, you gain valuable insight into mastering your depression. This empowers you to "get a handle" on your depression.

And the key to a healing path is found in

understanding the signs and symptoms that you utilize when you are sad. This book teaches you how to understand your own **depression profile** and therefore you <u>will</u> find a path for finding happiness.

The Symptoms of Depression Per Doctors

The National Institute of Health booklet (NIH Publication No. 11-3561 Revised 2011) states the symptoms of depression as:

- Persistent sad, anxious, or "empty" feelings

- Feelings of hopelessness or pessimism

- Feelings of guilt, worthlessness, or helplessness

- Irritability, restlessness

- Loss of interest in activities or hobbies once pleasurable, including sex

- Fatigue and decreased energy

- Difficulty concentrating, remembering details, and making decisions

- Insomnia, early-morning wakefulness, or excessive sleeping

- Overeating, or appetite loss

- Thoughts of suicide, suicide attempts

- Aches or pains, headaches, cramps, or digestive problems that do not ease even with treatment.

DECODING YOUR DEPRESSION SYMPTOMS

You might not realize this, but your body, soul, and mind are communicating your needs through your symptoms of depression.

Sexual Issues should be analyzed in regards to the nature of humanity: body, soul and mind.

Sex fills a distinct need in for each attribute of of a person. Valuable insight into finding happiness again when you know what your body gets from weeping – as well as your mind and soul.

I'm going to use the National Institute of Health's definitions and restructure them slightly into 'doing verbs' for the sake of this book. This certainly does not imply that I am a doctor! I am a writer with unique insight and personal experience with depression. My goal is to make it easier for you to figure out how to help yourself (this is a self-help book and not a medical journal after all!)

By turning these NIH symptoms into concrete actions, I researched books on all the symptoms of depression:

> Tears and Weeping
> Sex Issues
> Recurrent Dreams and Sleeplessness
> Rage
> Isolation and Withdrawal
> Fatigue and Ailments
> Confusion and Cognitive Issues
> Addictions
> Appetite Changes
> Dark Thoughts and Suicide

If everybody were the same, we would all have the same symptoms, right? However, each of these symptoms says something about your particular needs – it gives you clues about how your personality wants to heal itself from sadness.

Each symptom merits its own book so that readers can pick the symptoms that have personal meaning to them. Please look for my other books if you want to understand more about a particular symptom. They are all short and informative reads – and I get many compliments from readers on the help and support they find in the words.

A quick glance at the list shows that people have

an extremely flexible approach to sadness. Lumping every sad behavior under the vague umbrella of "depression" fails to decode your individual needs.

This errant approach is akin to blaming a scab for the initial cut! The scab – though painful – is evidence the body is healing from an injury. Preventing a scab by picking at it is absolutely the wrong medical advice. Trying to prevent the symptoms of depression – the tears, isolation, addictions, and etcetera – is like removing the scab from the wound and expecting a healing.

My new works explores your symptoms as a pattern of **healing** and not a demonstration of depression illness. Sexual Issues are not a sign you <u>are</u> depressed, rather sex problems are a sign of how your psyche <u>heals</u> from depression!

•••

Carl Jung used this same analytical philosophy for general personality traits. This led to such valuable tools as the Five Temperaments Model, the Keirsey Temperament Sorter and the Myers-Briggs Type Indicator. I am expanding upon Jung's early works about human temperaments, and making it granular (specifically to depression) so you can decode your depression profile.

Think again, about how different these two people are in dealing with depression:

Person A Exhibits Symptoms of:
Tears
Recurrent Dreams
Fatigue

~versus~

Person B Exhibits Symptoms of:
Rage
Isolation
Addiction

Using the same broad diagnosis of "depression" to such obviously different people – both of whom have amazingly different communication needs – is certainly bound to fail.

Depression Profiles help you clarify your needs by analyzing your unique pattern of processing sadness. Since knowledge is power, you gain dynamic insight into finding joy (even if the causative agent of depression does not change, such as my TBI injury).

Once you know what a symptom is asking of you,

you can cure yourself with intervention matching the need.

> If a child asks for a cup of water, do you give them a serpent?

If a depressed person has a symptom of crying, should they be treated for rage (or vice versa)?

MEDICAL REVIEW AND PERMISSION TO USE

I openly invite the medical community to test and review this concept of symptom based cure. I lack access to clinical methodology and large sample data. I know that the support of degreed expertise from capable physicians, academia, and scientists would cascade a tidal wave of recovery upon the shores of depression.

This brand new understanding of depression symptoms markedly changed me from a depression sufferer into a bestselling author and joyful individual. I am not free of the cares of this earth – but I am free from the crushing pressure of dark depression. I have great faith that this publication will greatly assist others in defeating depression as well. It would be nice to have the full support of the medical community to achieve recovery's full potential.

Now, to be very clear:

I am a supporter of physician prescribed medication and never want individuals to ignore any direction of a licensed medical professional.

This work is self-help, and not medical advice!

However, the concept of the Myers-Briggs has been widely tested and explored. Myers-Briggs in turn started with a pioneer thought, and a personal exploration of Carl Jung of his own dark side. I am merely standing on the shoulders of giants and applying the same concept of diagnostic granularity to the actual symptoms of depression.

Therefore, I give full and free permission to use this work in academic and behavioral studies. Outside of medical studies, I acknowledge the publicly beneficial rights of "Fair Use" rights, but I maintain copyright use of my own work. This is not public domain. (Play fair, be nice, and do not steal!)

Expected courtesy is to acknowledge Stephen Paul West, where it is due.

Email request for interviews and permission to use
to: Stephen@StephenPaulWest.com

CHAPTER 2

Sexual Issues and Depression

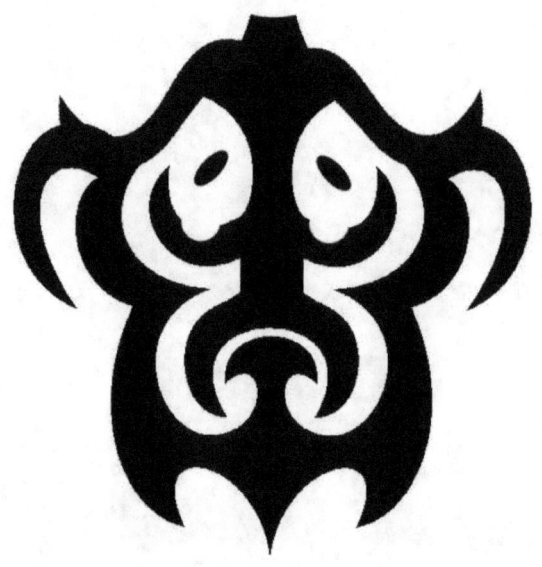

"γνῶθι σεαυτόν." That is, "Know Thyself" –Socrates; 400 B.C.

"There are three things extremely hard, Steel, a Diamond, and to know one's self." – Ben Franklin, Little Richard's 1750.

•●•

Decoding Your Symptoms

"Lost, I am. Lost…lost."

I stare up at the dark ceiling above me and whisper the words spontaneously. A moment ago, I was sound asleep. I did not even flinch when I awoke. I just woke up in the dead of night and whispering, "Lost I am. Lost…lost."

The silent ceiling does not reply. The house squats over me like a casket lid. I feel a few heartbeats before giant, hot breath exhales from the dark and pour crushing despair and anxiety into my lungs. Tears jump from the corners of my eyes.

I roll over and pull the blanket over my head. I am lost and I know it. I will not sleep again for three days. A strange anxiety just blew into my soul and denies me every comfort.

●●●

My books are very easy to use. Simply find your particular Symptom of Depression from the list and learn what that symptoms means.

Everybody has a different way of dealing with depression. The most common is weeping. However, if you put all your symptoms together you get a profile for how your body responds to sorrow. I call this the "<u>symptom matrix</u>".

We are all made up of a series of emotions. We all have unique symptoms. The ones above, in that moment in my dark room, were tears and sleeplessness. I would not be so lost in the future because I learned what those tears and sleeplessness symptoms were wanting.

You see, my body was telling me a clear message. I just did not have the training in how to hear, understand, and implement a solution. My <u>emotional immune response</u> of **tears** and sleeplessness gave me a **Depression Profile**.

You will also have symptoms. What are they?

Well? What are those symptoms Take this moment in time to reflect on how you process sorrow.

I am serious. Imagine your symptoms of depression as words swirling in front of your eyes.

I cannot answer what symptoms you have – but I

have the answers on what those symptoms mean.

You have to keep track of your symptoms. Write them down if necessary and then use this book to find that symptom and learn about its importance. Then put the solutions into action.

Easy!

So, my series on the meaning of depression symptoms have a regular pattern for convenience and consistency sake;

- An ancient and a modern quote and reference to the behavior showing its universality.

- A brief history of the symptom, including effects to The Body, The Mind and The Spirit as well as any relevant social commentary.

- The Pitfall of that Symptom

- The Strength of that Symptom

- Your take away and how to turn that symptoms into a solution!

I analyze every symptom using universally accepted interpretations of the symptom;

something Carl Jung called a "collective conscious". Therefore, an analysis might not hold rigidly true at an incident-by-incident microscopic level.

Sexual Issues are a symptom of depression – but not every performance issue is directly related to depression. Maybe you are just too tired for sex. Maybe your hormones are all messed up and you are way over hungry for too much sex. Just as dream interpretation fails people because not every moment in a dream is significant. However, the overall interpretation is very practical, and you will no doubt find great value by decoding your symptoms of depression. A single problem during sex is not significant – but weeks' worth of sexual failure is certainly significant.

I teach that your symptoms are actually paths of healing. That much is very true!

You say you have sexual problems in depression?
  • I say great! I know what that means!

You noticed you lost interest in physical intimacy
  • Wonderful, because now you will understand what those symptoms teach!

Feeling isolated?

- Excellent, this book helps you with that!

The symptoms of depression are good and very useful, once you identify and decode them individually. This work is an entire education in learning Depression Symptom cure.

•●•

There is a rich and fascinating history of every symptom of depression. However, prior to this innovative work, nobody pointed out clearly that these symptoms represent a body's preference for emotional healing. You will no doubt find the history of individual symptoms fascinating and valuable reading; just as I did doing the initial research. Where-ever possible, I provided outside clinical research data to support this work.

The <u>Weakness and Pitfall Section</u> analyzes the negatives of any particular symptom. Denoted by this serpent tattoo!

The <u>Strength Section</u> looks at the positives of any particular symptom. Denoted by this lion-warrior. Pow! Kiiiiyaaa!

Your plan of success teaches you to uncover the strengths to use ANY symptom of depression to your advantage. Denoted by this caduceus:

Some symptoms are self-apparently risky, such as suicide; but other symptoms are obviously less imminently dangerous. I found that I had a tendency just to try to hide my depression. You are your own best physician. Trust your own intellect in this matter, and do not talk yourself out of seeing a doctor when necessary.

A standard test is used by doctors to diagnose depression. It is called the Beck Depression Inventory, or BDI. This test has been around for a long time, so it's pretty accurate.

However, going to a doctor to get a test is not easy when you are depressed. Who wants to spend money on a test? We all just want to stay home and hide…and not add to our problems by spending $100s of dollars in testing to tell us the obvious.

The Beck Depression Inventory (BDI) is copyrighted and requires a physician for proper application. It was cost prohibitive for me to schedule a BDI on a constant basis. I knew I was depressed – and I wanted to get a cure and not get a diagnosis and a little poorer.

My single day costs for being run over was over $38,000 – and rapidly climbed to over $88,000 in a single week. Financial pressure just adds to the bitterness of depression.

Great news though! This book is inexpensive (recklessly cheap given the thousands of hours I put into writing it *grin*)

My book does not crush you beneath a mountain of expenses. I truly understand sorrow and depression. I am truly interested in helping you!

> "Hey," a girlfriend asked. "I sent you a card. Did you like it?"

> "I… um… I don't like going to the mailbox. So, I stopped."

> "That's crazy. Everybody checks their mailbox."

> "Why? Why would I check my mailbox? It's

only filled with bad news. Medical bills. Threats. Confusing stuff. So I stopped. I will never go to the mailbox again."

"Oh…" she looks around a minute. I can tell she is tossed back and forth between feeling hurt I ignored her card, shock at my insane solution to bills, and pity that I am crazy enough to think it's a workable solution. "Well," she finally says realizing I am just a lost guy with a messed up head injury, "I will send you something sweet every week. Why don't you go and check?"

"Sure," I reply, but know that I do not intend to check that mailbox. Finding a sweet card in a mountain of medical bills is not enough enticement to make me get my mail.

Those who are accident victims understand that bills just add to sexual frustration. Its not possible to find a date-night when our finances are in ruin from doctor's bills.

Bullies would like to say we deserve to be impoverished because we did not manage our money. Well, the fact is that life sometimes gangs up on you and runs you over with a vehicle and drops a $88,000 dollar debt in your life.

Visits & Claims - Medical Claim Summary

■ Recently finalized ▣ In process ■ Finalized

Claims

DATE OF VISIT ▼	PATIENT NAME	PHYSICIAN / PROVIDER	My Responsibility	TOTAL CHARGES
02/02/2	STEPHEN W	DAUGHTERS OF CHARITY HEALTH	$23,631.00	$23,631.00
02/02/20	STEPHEN WI	PETROLEUM HELICOPTERS INC	$12,737.00	$12,737.00
02/02/2	STEPHEN WI	AUSTIN PATHOLOGY ASSOCIATES	$53.00	$53.00
02/02/7	STEPHEN WI	AUSTIN PATHOLOGY ASSOCIATES	$53.00	$53.00
02/02/2	STEPHEN WI	DAUGHTERS OF CHARITY HEALTH	$720.00	$720.00
02/02/20	STEPHEN WI	AUSTIN RADIOLOGICAL ASSOC	$204.00	$204.00
02/02/2	STEPHEN WI	AUSTIN RADIOLOGICAL ASSOC	$128.00	$128.00
02/02/20	STEPHEN W	AUSTIN RADIOLOGICAL ASSOC	$37.00	$37.00
02/02/20	STEPHEN W	AUSTIN RADIOLOGICAL ASSOC	$309.00	$309.00
02/02/20	STEPHEN WI	AUSTIN RADIOLOGICAL ASSOC	$266.00	$266.00
02/02/20	STEPHEN WI	AUSTIN RADIOLOGICAL ASSOC	$309.00	$309.00

By using Sexual Issues and Depression you empower yourself to rapidly understand all your healing needs. This is both life-saving and inexpensive. My work makes a huge difference – especially if you are facing a huge medical expense like me. The guy who left me dead and bloody on the road never paid a dime! Talk about depression-based rage, tears, and dark thoughts!

YOUR DEPRESSION SOLUTION IN THIS BOOK

Nobody asks more questions about their behavior than the depressed. "Why do I cry so much? Why do I isolate myself from all my friends?" and so on.

Lots of why's. The answer always comes back from the medical community: "Because you are depressed."

But is that answer correct? "Doctors say I cry because I am depressed." (Substitute any other symptom of depression and the answer is always the same.)

Can the answer to each of these symptoms really be the same? Obviously not. Look at how different they all are:

- Tears and Weeping
- Sex Issues
- Recurrent Dreams and Sleeplessness
- Rage
- Isolation and Withdrawal
- Fatigue and Ailments
- Confusion and Cognitive Issues
- Addictions
- Appetite Changes
- Dark Thoughts and Suicide

However, let me ask: Does the body weep to be depressed, or to be healed of depression?

Did the light turn on? Do you see the major difference in the approach to your symptoms of depression? Would the human body waste time on doing something that served NO purpose in preserving the organism?

I want you to be happy. I do not want your symptoms to be part of the mystery of your depression. Your symptoms are pointing towards healing. I know you will find your path of happiness.

The mere fact you are reading this book shows that you want to be well, happy, and empowered.

Healing from a deep cut requires a process that includes; bleeding, blood clotting, shock, an immune system response, a scab, and lastly a scar. These are all physical <u>SYMPTOMS</u> of the body healing a wound. The physical symptoms represent a healing process of the body.

A scab is a symptom of healing. A scar is a symptom of the cut – but these are NOT causing the cut. It's obvious to us all that physical immune responses don't CAUSE the cut.

So, why do people say that sexual issues is depression? **Why do we medicate against the symptoms of depression…** instead of acknowledging that rage, isolation and even suicidal thoughts are NOT depression, but an emotional immune response. There are 10 basic responses to depression. The body is trying to get over depression by showing these signs.

In similar harmony, emotional healing of your mind, body, and soul requires that the symptoms of depression are manifest. These symptoms are individually unique and show you how to recover from depression.

The symptoms are not causing your depression.

The symptoms are good, and are trying to heal you from depression.

Being afraid of them is like being afraid of a scab after a cut. Something else is causing the symptoms of depression, some other root cause, and your body is picking what it considers an appropriate symptomatic response to the sorrow.

Yes, the body weeps to purge depression. What about all the other symptoms? Things like rage, sex issues, or isolation? There are 10 unique symptoms of depression – and each symptoms combines with others to show you something on purpose. What about them?

Until my work, there has not been a specific look at what a person is subconsciously communicating via their personal symptoms of depression.

●●●

One of the great failures of Sigmund Freud was his over reliance on symbolism. He felt if you had a head ache then somebody had said something hurtful about you; if a person was nauseous then they could not "stomach something".

Freud erred in minimizing the link set of

symptoms that were diagnostically significant. He short-circuited most of his psychoanalyses because he interpreted symptoms as mere symbols of inner desires. However, the same errors of neglect are still being made with depression. Fortunately, modern psychoanalysis has walked away from Freud's too simplistic and inaccurate view of symptoms.

However, depression also needs a new review of the symptoms.

Just as modern psychoanalysis has dismissed much of Freud's early work in favor of more detailed analysis, the same process must be done with the symptoms of depression.

In fact, I believe all the symptoms of depression are not simply "indicators that you are depressed", but are in fact, demonstrative of how your body, mind, and soul want to heal from depression. This is not just a subtle difference between current views about depression and the symptoms.

This is a pioneering statement of empowerment!

Understand your symptoms to find your cure for depression.

Society In Search of Healing

As a modern society, we spend no time decoding how we mourn. Symptoms are lumped into a gooey mass called depression.

> "Look at that stupid blue umbrella hopping behind that woman! How the hell is that depression! A cute little cartoon umbrella and a cryin' woman looking out a window? Oh, on a rainy day. The rain must make it depressing. Stupid! Baaaa"

> I turned off the TV in disgust and just sit there, smoldering in a weird funk. My dog looks up at me and wags a tail a bit.

> "That's not depression," I explain to my furry friend. "Depression is ugly and dark. It's filled with rage and anger and death. It's certainly not a stupid blue umbrella. Depression is death."

> My collie stretches out and ignores my ranting. He is used to it. People, though. Well, they are pretty much freaked out by my fast changing temperament.

> "Umbrella? Stupid. BS. That's why I don't watch TV."

Even my dog had enough. He gets up and wanders outside. I sit there another half hour cursing that damn umbrella. What does a cartoon know about the kind of depression that stalks me? Nothing. My rage is real – the umbrella is the work of fiction.

Some attempt might be made to categorize the type of depression (i.e.: post-partum, teen, manic, bi-polar, etc.) In turn, that categorized label of depression is thrown onto the back of the sorrowful. Perhaps some pills are prescribed to treat a particular category of depression. In best cases, a great physician gets involved. But, I bet it is accurate to say 95% of depression cases are sent on their way with nothing more than the clothes on their back. Too bad? Or, just plain cruel?

Our society is almost afraid to look deeply into our own eyes. It's as if we feel it is perverse to be romantically interested in our soul. Strangely, history is replete with stories of people and societies in search of themselves. Plato and Socrates did not invent the phrase, "know thyself"; it is simply that their words managed to survive for over two thousand years in written form.

However, every creed is searching for the answer to this hard question. It is the question of the

"Why is there pain?" For each person, this search initially takes an infantile view of judging the world. Just as an infant expects a caring adult to answer every cry, so a spiritual infant expects God to answer every cry. However, once we are mature we realize that screaming our demands yields no benefit – and is, in fact, rather embarrassing.

In similar light, the mature path for every spiritual journey eventually arrives at one's self. We cannot change the world. Often, we cannot even find an excuse for the crazy evil that so randomly befalls in the world. However, each of us can, and must, realize that we control our emotions – and even then only to the limits of human pathos.

This painful journey has led me to an important discovery that all symptoms of depression are actually a method of healing.

At first, I blamed everybody (especially the nameless, faceless, criminal who ran me over and left me for dead). Ultimately, I realized that even though I was correct in blaming others, it did nothing to make me whole. I did not start healing correctly until I looked at each incident of crying, or rage, or isolation, or murderous thought. I had every symptom of depression. Yet, I learned to master each symptom when I learned to evaluate it

102

properly, and then feed the healing component of that symptom.

●●●

Symptoms of depression do not all mean the same thing. Let's make up some imaginary depressed people. I just randomly picked a few symptoms out of the 10 for this illustration. Think again about these two people diagnosed with depression.

How are these individuals different?

<u>Person C:</u>
Sleeplessness
Fatigue
Isolation

~versus~

<u>Person D:</u>
Rage
Addiction
Isolation

In this case, I gave both hypothetical individuals "Isolation" as a common symptom. And yet, you can easily see that Person C has an entirely different set of healing needs than Person D.

The symptoms of depression are clearly unique biological paths to healing. Each person has different needs. Therefore, each person has different symptoms.

But the symptoms are TELLING you something very important. I teach you how to listen to your symptoms and get better.

HOW DOCTORS DECIDE YOU HAVE DEPRESSION

I have already referenced the Myers-Briggs Type Indicator; but I did so without explanation. I want to take a moment to explain the technology, as well as look at the various other analytical tools such as the Glasgow Extended Scale for TBI, and the Beck Depression Inventory.

People are not machines, not software, and not robots

Analogies are made between the pulleys on a robot and the tendons in a body. That does not make humans into machines. So any analytical tool applied to human beings must remain flexible enough to adapt to very complex variables.

Modern tools of Analytical Psychology must reflect a necessary flexibility. Carl Jung developed a view of human behavior that indicated some predictability in human preferences. During WWII, Katharine Cook Briggs and her daughter, Isabel Briggs Myers expanded his work in the hopes of best matching women workers to a job.

Subsequently, the Myers-Briggs test has grown to

become the largest personality test in the world.

These personality tests are extensively used by business to identify communication styles and relationship needs. The idea is that once a person has knowledge of their personality style, they have a superior mastery of their work environment. Myers-Briggs helps people discover themselves – a self-diagnostic tool. It does not magically pick the best job field for a person (as originally proposed in the 1940s).

In fact, bosses who think some test is going to give them magical control over their staff are a little delusional. But, it is fun to know a little about yourself – so I enjoy taking these things just to 'know myself'. Plato would be proud!

However, when your body is communicating something directly about your depression – well, that is some important information. Depression symptoms can also be analyzed to discover the style of healing your body needs to be happy again. This analysis is much deeper than using the Myers-Briggs for a job, and it yields huge benefits to you, the depression sufferer.

Depression symptoms are an 'emotional immune response' to depression injury, and the weeping, rage, or other emotions are the body's response to the internal injury of sorrow.

So, just like Rosie the Riveter you are powerful.

Carl Jung empowered women in the workforce in the 1940's

A picture of Rose Monroe, a real-life Rosie the Riveter in the 1940s.

We Can Do It!

The patriotic World War II poster of the fictional Rosie representing the female workforce during the war.

Compared to Myers-Briggs, a more clinically refined tool was necessary for evaluating traumatic brain injuries (TBI). For example, in the real world of combat injuries the US Military has a field test for TBI. Some soldiers who do not want to be removed from the field have learned the proper answers and fake "healthy" in brain injury tests. For those with Brain Injuries the standard tool for evaluation is called a Glasgow Outcome Scale (GOS). When it was originally created, it was so broad as to be only marginally useful. It had (5) possibilities running from "Dead", "Vegetative", so on, up to "Good Recovery".

This scale originally let a medical professional sort out the brain injured victims in a crude triage fashion. It was useful because it was applied at time of injury, at 3 months, then at 6 months and again at 12 months. **This kind of healing time is important for the reader to note.** Recovery from depression takes time – this is especially true when accompanied by physical injury.

However, the original Glascow Outlook Scale was criticized as being too broad, and it was improved to become the GOS-Expanded by adding additional granularity.

That phrase of "granularity" is also how I explain my Sexual Issues and Depression. It is my opinion that the diagnosis of "depression" is too broad, and that much valuable insight is lost when not looking at each depression symptoms in detail.

•●•

Drilling down into the world of Depression there is a common clinical test called the Beck Depression Inventory (BDI). This test of 21 questions allows a doctor to score how depressed an individual feels. This is important as the doctor gains quick insight into the status of the unhappiness of a patient. Naturally, it is not 100% accurate. Clinical testing shows it is about 90% accurate, because it is impossible to turn human behavior into pulleys and software.

For example, after my injury, I was frightened of having people see me as different. Even though I was brain injured, I was smart enough to pick the best answer in order to make me seem healthy. In reality, I was too scared and anxious to be honest. I was one of those 10% of people who threw off the Beck Depression Inventory.

So, the BDI measures the depth and intensity of depression in patients with psychiatric diagnoses. The BDI has extensive clinical value, and has measured the "how much" a person is depressed since its original creation in 1961 by Aaron Beck.

However, my work drills down not into just the "how much" of depression, nor the clinical "what type of depression", but the "what healing you need to be happy". Obviously, the cure is best and it is found by taking a serious analytical view of the symptoms of sorrow you display.

My Sexual Issues and Depression is different than the medical diagnoses of what type of depression a person experiences (such as post-partum, teen, or the many important diagnostic information as found in the Diagnostic and Statistical Manual of Mental Disorders DSM-IV by the American Psychiatric Association).

My goal creates a tool of self-help for depression that combines the valuable insight of something like Myer-Briggs with the granularity of the GOS and BDI.

The clinical evaluation of my symptom analysis works for me. I am forgetting how to be depression. I am forgetting depression. No longer am I lost – instead its my depression that is lost. Nice – and so can you.

You alone will answer for yourself. You alone are responsible for yourself. However, in the hands of dedicated readers this pioneering work is a valuable convalescent tool. It would be impossible to be 100% accurate, just like the BDI cannot be

100% accurate, but its value is self-evident.

I do not feel badly that I am putting the onerous on you for healing. I am sure you agree that 95% of depressed people get NO support what-so-ever. My tool is invaluable for filling that huge gap of need.

It would be foolish for me to say, "If you cry it always means exactly this-and-that." But, it is more foolish for a medical doctor to say, "Your tears just mean you're depressed. Your rage just means you are depressed. Your isolation just means you are depressed. Your dark thoughts just mean you are depressed. Etcetera ad nauseam"

Does every symptom merit the broad stroke of "It just means you're depressed?"

Absolutely not.

Rather, individual symptoms indicate how the body wants individual healing.

> NOTE: Rage, Suicide, and Addiction need immediate medical help no matter how much, how little, or any other factors of depression.

My goal is for you to heal yourself from

depression. I see this work as a tool to assist you in your quest; a tool that has many other important counter-parts including physicians and medication.

The chapter plan of action and the symptom cure are denoted with the Caduceus Tribal image that I designed for this book.

All the tribal images are my design and I think they perfectly express the mystery of power that is found in harmonizing depression in our lives. Most of the are in this book is mine, and I found making art and writing cure depression too.

In most images, you can find a hidden representation of a human soul. I liked the mystery and found it a fun way to illustrate this work.

People need help.

My work helps the inquisitive and curious. My artwork and illustrations are a fun way to decode a serious issue. It is important you learn to harmonize your depression. I hope this work helps you greatly!

Do not substitute this book for a proper physical and mental checkup. This work is an important tool – but it takes more than a single tool to build a house. It takes many tools to learn to harmonize depression as well.

FIND YOUR SYMPTOMS OF DEPRESSION

If you want to use the Depression Matrix immediately just find the short books related to the symptoms you feel. It is refreshing for people to put together their own knowledge base.

I realize that you may have any and all of the symptoms. I have the complete works all together in my more expensive "Sexual Issues and Depression" but these works are shorter, easier to read and cost hardly anything.

Just research each select the little book you need. Combine each symptom together to get a "depression profile". Actually, once you have an idea of your symptoms you can call it a "**healing profile**" because that is exactly how you should use Sexual Issues and Depression.

Every symptom of depression is a path of healing!

You can research your particular style(s) of mourning:

- Tears and Weeping
- Sex Issues
- Recurrent Dreams and Sleeplessness
- Rage
- Isolation and Withdrawal
- Fatigue and Ailments
- Confusion and Cognitive Issues
- Addictions
- Appetite Changes
- Dark Thoughts and Suicide

You might notice there is no particular order to the symptoms. I avoided the sterile presentation of alphabetical organization for a reason. In similar fashion, I did not pile them up in order of severity. My reason for this is I want the reader to be flexible.

I do not want a formulaic approach to decoding yourself. Be flexible. Be creative. Believe in yourself to be smart enough to know your own self. You are in charge of you!

I also did not want to make the book more and more alarming by rolling up the more serious symptoms of depression in a steadily advancing progression. In other words, I didn't want the last three books to be Rage, Addictions, and Suicide. Holy moly, putting those 3 altogether would scare anybody!

However, I think we can all agree that "Crying" as compared to "Suicide" are not in the same arena of risk. This book is a work of common sense as much as it is a pioneering belief that the symptoms of depression are actually healing processes in disguise.

Depression is a flexible creature and I do not want to over-organize the process for the reader. I want the reader to be nimble, flexible and to use that overly active depression-base analysis for some good!

Remember earlier, I said I want you to get well and happy. I want you to know yourself. I do not want your symptoms to be part of the mystery of your depression. Your symptoms are pointing you towards healing. I believe you can, and will, find your path of happiness.

The mere fact you are reading this book shows that you WANT to be well, happy, and empowered. Those who seek most often find.

UTILIZING YOUR PROFILE

Finally, once you looked at all your symptoms you can now compile a list of your strengths for each symptom. I found this amazingly beneficial. Obviously, once you understand the positive for a symptom you can maximize its benefit.

For each Symptom I mark the strength of that symptom with this tribal image below:

It is a lion up of two warriors facing each other.

Every strength has a weakness (this is not just a cliché for Kung-Fu movies). So I outline some of the important weaknesses you need to guard against.

The weakness section for each chapter is marked as a Pitfall and I used a snake (i.e. a "Pit" viper) to represent the risk.

People are not always kind. In fact, some people are predators and see weaknesses as a point of exploitation. Being knowledgeable of any pitfall is definitely in your own self-interest. You cannot heal depression if you cannot make yourself safe and secure.

Healing starts from a safe, secure, and protected place.

Consider the shelter of a womb, or the fact that military nursing stations are far from the sound of the battle front. This self-preservation needs to be part of your healing plan.

Enjoy the book.

May you find it enlightening.

May you find it healing.

SUMMARY

I found that I weaved and bobbed through these symptoms. I found that some things would make me weep but others would make me enraged – still others might make me retreat.

Yes, it is very possible to have several symptoms all at once.

It is possible that one event can make you respond with a unique symptom of depression and another event might make you display a different symptom. For example, you might weep if your kids hurt you, but become enraged if a stranger hurts you. You can see the different symptoms are manifesting different needs in these examples.

Just combine all the needs and plans of action if you have many symptoms at once.

- Tears and Weeping
- Sex Issues
- Recurrent Dreams and Sleeplessness
- Rage
- Isolation and Withdrawal
- Fatigue and Ailments

- Confusion and Cognitive Issues
- Addictions
- Appetite Changes
- Dark Thoughts and Suicide

For example, often I would combine the symptom of weeping, dreams and isolation. If you review these books, you will see the symptoms harmonize – the common thread is a need for safe communication and effective plan of action.

In my case, because I did not feel safe, it forced me into isolation. Yes, I did need a confidant to share my heart – but no, I did not have that person. So I became Isolated and had a lot of Recurrent Dreams and Sleeplessness. Obviously, my mind was processing the pain. However, once I figured it out I worked hard to find a doctor I truly trusted. I stopped talking with people who did not get my pain – they were just dismissive and added to the depression. I figured out a way to make my nightmares stop.

You will also find that proper diet and rest is necessary to resolve all the symptoms of depression.

Two surprising common solutions are exercise and being kind to others. Statistics show if you add exercise and you do good deeds for others, then it greatly improves your depression.

So, here is the meaning of all the symptoms:

Tears and Weeping
Tears demonstrate a need to notify other people of our pain. It is a social S.O.S. asking for help. When you cry, your subconscious is asking for help, empathy, and outside support. If you can safely meet that need, without judgment, it will help you heal.

Sex Issues
Sex Issues represents a need to prioritize energy needs during recovery. During depression, the mind often consumes all available energy in problem solving and healing. This does not leave energy available to regulate hormones, blood flow and arousal. For single people it is important to find the harmony with your mind – and be social but celibate. Couples need to plan for intimacy and have open dialogues as you recover.

Recurrent Dreams and Sleeplessness
Recurrent Dreaming is a matter of processing recent memories. Your mind is working out the details of what is important, and this is good. This symptom of depression means you desire a plan of

action. Furthermore, it demonstrates your ability to find a solution and come to terms. The solution is to deliberately and consciously identify the fear during waking hours and then attach another little positive idea to that existing fear.

Rage

Rage represents the limits of your mind's ability to cope with daily pressures. Rage is a "hard edge" that tells you that you need to reduce input and demands on your system. Depression based rage is telling you that you lack adequate room for healing time. Rage is not blind-stupidity; it is communicating clear mental-resource needs. It is your job to step back and listen.

Isolation and Withdrawal

Isolation represents a need for your body, mind and spirit to fall back and regroup in order to formulate a solution. It is a "strong defense" that provides the environment you need for analytical thinking. Isolation is not a failure to socialize, but an optimal environment for you to solve the puzzle of depression. It is your job to implement your solutions once formulated; and pull yourself out of isolation when ready.

Fatigue and Ailments

Fatigue represents an accumulation of stresses –

both physical and mental – that has pushed your body into a failure mode. It is a strong reaction to depression, that demonstrates you are not listening to your biological needs closely enough; and you need to focus on your health on a consistent long-term plan to reduce the stress to a level your body and mind accepts as tolerable. There is no short-term fix as it requires you rebuild trust between your conscious and subconscious self.

Confusion and Cognitive Issues

Confusion represents a need for the mind to resolve issues, reorganize life events, and develop a healthy nutrition plan for metabolic performance. During depression, the mind becomes very analytical and this consumes large amounts of resources. At the extreme spectrum of memory issues there is a marked reduction of intellectual capacity, but typical cognitive issues are more internally perceived than actually debilitating in reality.

Addictions

Addictions represent a need for pleasurable reward for your body, mind or spirit – possibly all three. Since we are organo-chemical creatures, we respond rapidly to chemical influences, which in turn change our perceptions. Addictions have a cruel way of taking over a life, however, and leaving a person destroyed in the end. It is best to identify what rewards is satisfied by the addiction, and find another means of meeting the same rewards in a safe manner.

Appetite Changes

Appetite Changes represent an empowerment of control and also represents a change in energy needs. Fasting means the brain wants more clean fuel. Indulgence means your body wants an easy fuel. Appetite changes are an energy equation with some social influence.

Dark Thoughts and Suicide

Dark thoughts and suicidal ideation represent a need to find a safe-place from pain. Our minds will consider all ideas for removing pain, and therefore it will visit dark ideas. However, you cannot reduce your pain by creating hurt to yourself or others. You must identify a positive approach to managing your pain by creating a safe-place; this place may include the body, the mind, or the spirit.

You will notice that all the symptoms are actually manifestations of needs – and this shows you a plan of healing.

In each short diagnostic book, I have a plan of

action to maximize the benefits of any particular symptom. Please review those plans at the end the books for any symptom you are processing.

Here are links to the various plans to use any symptom as a SOLUTION to sorrow:

> Tears and Weeping Plan
> Sex Issues Plan
> Recurrent Dream Plan
> Rage Plan
> Isolation and Withdrawal Plan
> Fatigue and Ailment Plan
> Confusion and Cognitive Issues Plan
> Addiction Plan
> Appetite Changes Plan
> Overcoming Dark Thoughts and Suicide Plan

It is not possible to live on a mountain top always. The air is too thin, there is no food. A person must come down to the valley occasionally for supplies.

So it is that it is not always possible to be always happy.

Depression is VERY useful and not to be feared. Many good things come out of depression – the most obvious being a serious consideration of the realities of living. We are more thoughtful, analytical, and cautious during depression. This is depression's job!

However, by running away from the symptoms we are failing to see depression as a tool for healing.

My work, Sexual Issues and Depression is a pioneering work into the obvious. You can totally harmonize your depression and rule it by using the information in this work.

I truly am very sorry you have been injured. I wish it had never happened to you.

Much love.

Much peace.

Much joy and healing to you.

The End

Stephen Paul West is a best-selling novelist living in Austin Texas.

Crying and Depression

This short book is a deep dive into the meaning of tears. There are 10 major symptoms of depression. Reach each of these exciting books to solve your individual symptom of depression.

Top Ten Cures for Sciatica and Back Pain

Healing at the Speed of Read! Fix your back pain fast.

A list of ten 'must haves' to cure sciatica and back pain. Recovery from lower back pain and injury is difficult. This short self-help book presents the most powerful and effective ways to get pain relief fast! It is the ten best cures to recover from lower back injury and sciatic.

The Peace of Gaza

The Peace of Gaza. Shocking. Stunning and Beautiful. This powerful story reveals how the Gaza Strip can finally find real and lasting peace. Prepare to be touched to your core. Three souls wander the very place where twenty years earlier the world was ending.

Women Slaves of War

A true story. A biographical-fiction base on three women who were caught in modern civil wars. Motherhood on the point of extinction. Modern warfare has no rules, no honor, and everywhere women pay the highest costs; their children sacrificed to the dogs of war.

Extortion Politics and the Federal Shutdown

The mighty United States of America brought to a halt by a zealous group with a narrow agenda of absolute control. Is this a plot for a new conspiracy movie? Is this the act of foreign terrorists?

No. Just a single little vindictive lobbyist. Grover.

Rise of the Maiden - Blood and Venom

Craving something new and sophisticated in the paranormal genre? Rise of the Maiden - Blood and Venom series will give you a glimpse into paranormal culture not yet explored.

In the first years of the reign of Victoria, an infant girl is stolen from the dirty streets of London. For fifteen years she is held an unknowing prisoner by the captor she calls 'father'.

Depression Symptoms Decoded

The cure for depression is found in the symptoms that are displayed. Symptoms are a body's immune response to emotional damage. This is the complete work of all the short works on depression symptoms.

The body has a method to heal emotional injury and this includes Weeping, Sex Issues, Recurrent Dreams, Rage, Isolation, Fatigue, Confusion, Addictions, Appetite Changes and Dark Thoughts/Suicide.